LAST YEARS of the CLASS 50s 1980-1994

ISBN 978-1-913390-96-9
Strathwood
4 Shuttleworth Road,
Elm Farm Industrial Estate,
Bedford
MK41 0EP
Printed via Akcent Media Limited

Telephone: 01234 328792

Cover: Thumping past our cameraman 50037 Illustrious takes the Salisbury line at Battledown Flyover with the 14.37 Basingstoke to Exeter service, which today had started at nearby Basingstoke because of re-signalling work taking place at Waterloo, on 30 March 1991. *Rail Photoprints*

Previous Page: Looking less than pleased, 50034 Furious will soon be no more as staff from Cooper's Metals slice up the unfortunate locomotive by the turntable at Old Oak Common in early February 1991. *Strathwood Library Collection*

Below: Stepping away nicely from Charlbury on 16 May 1986, 50045 Achilles works the 07.00 Hereford to Paddington 'Cathedrals Express'. This viewpoint was so open in the 1980s that Walcot Farm Cottages on the Charlbury to Burford road can be seen in the distance. *Martin Loader*

Class 50s – A Photographic Tribute

Barrie Renwick was born in Haltwhistle, in February 1952. Whilst still a youngster, his family moved to Hull, where he would remain for the rest of his life. When he was a child, Barrie used to push pencils along the floor, pretending they were trains, and this is where his interest in railways began. Like most railway enthusiasts, Barrie started off as a train spotter, but this rapidly took a back seat, when he acquired his first camera in the early 1970s. His hobby was mainly confined to the UK, but his interests were in all types of motive power, steam, diesel, and electric. However, regarding mainline traction, it was generally the English Electric types of Classes 37, 40, 50, and 55 which he admired the most. I first met Barrie when I was staying at a guest house in Dawlish in September 1986. Soon becoming good friends with a common interest, we went on railway holidays together for the next fifteen years. In the evenings, we would enjoy slide shows, and down the years I would be treated to all his images, past and present. He had learned his craft at the Hull Photographic Society and was also a member of the RCTS and several heritage railways too. From 1978, his pictures were taken on a Canon AE1 camera, but having accidently left this on a train in the first half of 1990, he purchased a Canon EOS camera in July 1990, which he used until at least 2004. Most of his images were taken using Kodachrome 64 film.

Barrie was something of a perfectionist, and with his photographs he strived for correct exposure, accurate composition, and so on. He preferred sunny images and was not a fan of taking (or looking at) slides taken on dull days, "What is the point?", he once said to me. On numerous occasions I had suggested that we could possibly approach a publishing company, with a view to writing a

book together. "You've got to be known" was always his reply, somebody like Colin Marsden, John Vaughan, Les Nixon, Gavin Morrison, and many others who we admired greatly. So, we never pursued it any further, and Barrie's photos were to remain private, until he sadly passed away suddenly in January 2018, aged 65. I hope that Barrie's photos in this second publication after Last Years of the Deltics 1977-1982, and any future ones, provide the reader with great satisfaction, they are now a lasting tribute not only to his memory, but also to his ability as a talented photographer.

Guy Wood
Coventry

Two splendid views to demonstrate the photographic eye of the late Barrie Renwick taken on 5 June 1980 at Dawlish. It seems that although it appears to be bright and sunny there might perhaps still be a little chill in the air this morning from the appearance of those folk out early enough to watch 50002 Superb set off again from her station stop with a Liverpool to Plymouth service. Then again soon after as 50005 Collingwood slips by almost unnoticed with an up parcels working. **Both: Barrie Renwick**

Later the same day and it is now warming up nicely as can be seen by the family strolling the seawall at Dawlish, as they pause to watch the passage of 50006 Neptune tasked today with a Paddington to Plymouth express. *Barrie Renwick*

Opposite: Staying in the area we return two days later on 7 June 1980 to record 50046 Ajax looking nice and clean working today's St. Austell to Kensington Olympia motorail service, provided for those holidaymakers who perhaps hated the traffic jams to get to their chosen holiday destination but perhaps still wanted the luxury and comfort of their car to be able to tour Cornwall.
Barrie Renwick

Opposite: Not so many photographers have used the footbridge by Starcross station as their vantage point it seems, however Barrie has done us proud with this view of 50034 Furious with a Penzance to Birmingham duty, once again well-presented but still a while to go before her refurbishment in the autumn of 1982. *Barrie Renwick*

Having an eye for a picture and some human activity unaware of the camera always helps a scene, such as this one at Dawlish Warren on 12 June 1980 as 50011 Centurion has been given clear signals for the through line with her Birmingham to Plymouth working. *Barrie Renwick*

Having arrived at Penzance together on 19 September 1980, 50037 Illustrious and 50016 Barham have been given the dolly signal to move forward light engine towards the signal box before being stabled alongside the station. *Barrie Renwick*

The platform ends at Bristol Temple Meads is our next stop on 17 April 1981 to enjoy the appearance of 50008 Thunderer arriving with a Liverpool to Penzance service. *Barrie Renwick*

Having been just refurbished in March 1981, 50035 Ark Royal heads west away from Dawlish with a Paddington to Penzance past the busy looking beach on 4 September 1981. She was one of forty-four of the class to be sent straight out in the attractive Large Logo livery after their refurbishment work was completed at Doncaster Works. *Barrie Renwick*

The next day we are on the footbridge at Dawlish Warren to watch 50011 Centurion pass underneath us with a noticeably short rake making up a Wolverhampton to Penzance train. In time she would be the first Class 50 to be withdrawn on 24 February 1987. Finally, after a long time of being dumped at Crewe Works, she was scrapped there by Texas Metals in September 1992. **Barrie Renwick**

Opposite: The appearance of 50018 Resolution which has just arrived off the Southern Region from Waterloo at her journey's end Exeter St. David's on 9 September 1981, leaves a little to be desired with still a further fifteen months to go before a return to traffic in Large Logo livery after her full refurbishment.
Barrie Renwick

The lower quadrant signal is off for the passage of a down train soon to cross 50025 Invincible heading east from Dawlish with a Plymouth to Paddington service on 12 September 1981, likewise 50025 was itself eleven months away from full refurbishment.
Barrie Renwick

Opposite: The use of a telephoto lens for effect rather than out of habit has been put to good use to capture 50013 Agincourt at Aller Junction on Saturday 12 September 1981 with the Motorail service from Kensington Olympia bound for St. Austell. As it is getting late in the season there appears to still be some spare capacity for cars remaining.
Barrie Renwick

Leaning into the curve on the approaches to Teignmouth station the following day 13 September 1981, 50037 Illustrious puts in another appearance, this time at the head of Paddington to Plymouth service.
Barrie Renwick

Opposite: This is a location on the seafront at Dawlish that works well for light engine portrait shots with the sun in the right direction, as here on 17 September 1981 to record the passage of 50004 St. Vincent heading west. The locomotive's Large Logo livery looks somewhat sooty now eleven months after being refurbished at Doncaster Works. *Barrie Renwick*

The somewhat less photogenic surroundings of New Street station in Birmingham is our next location the following spring, as our replacement driver for the refurbished 50040 Leviathan in April 1982 strolls towards us. She had taken up this name in September 1978, although she would be re-named as Centurion from July 1987. *David T. Williams*

Left: Un-refurbished 50014 Warspite rolls into Charlbury with the 16.33 Paddington to Hereford service on 16 May 1982, just before most trains on this route were replaced with units. *Martin Loader*

Below: On 28 July 1982, 50050 Fearless approaches Bodmin Road with a Liverpool to Penzance duty which it has brought from Birmingham. *Barrie Renwick*

Another Liverpool to Penzance inter-regional working is signalled through on the fast line through Dawlish Warren on 10 September 1982 behind 50005 Collingwood. She would be fitted with a crest embellishment from the Royal Navy on 21 November 1987 in a ceremony at Paddington. HMS Collingwood does not go to sea but is in fact the onshore base in Fareham established in 1940 for new recruits into the navy. The plethora of fine lower quadrant semaphore signals were still controlled from the signal box almost opposite our cameraman's position at this time.
Barrie Renwick

Looking smart in Large Logo livery if we ignore the sooty deposits of course, 50025 Invincible will now start to accelerate the 11.10 Waterloo to Exeter away from the speed restrictions around Clapham Junction on 16 September 1982. She had become the twenty-eighth of her class to be refurbished and sent out in this new attractive livery only a month beforehand. *Rail Photoprints*

Surrounded by Cotswold dry stone walls, 50034 Furious passes Coate, between Stroud and Kemble with the 09.15 Gloucester to Swindon parcels on 30 April 1983. Despite the line having been converted to colour light signalling many years before, the steam age telegraph poles still survived into the 1980s at this location. *Martin Loader*

Setting off from Moreton-in-Marsh station on 9 April 1983, 50029 Renown has the 07.05 Hereford to Paddington service. In this view all the trappings of a traditional GWR station were still to be seen, goods shed, semaphore signals, signal box, station building, old world charm indeed. *Martin Loader*

Opposite: Passing Hinksey Yard with the 15.15 Oxford to Paddington on 28 July 1983, 50047 Swiftsure being just the fifth of the class to be refurbished was returned to Western Region service still in her Rail Blue livery in May 1980. The move to Large Logo livery in this case only came about in early 1984. **Martin Loader**

Right: The choice a telephoto lens works well again here for this composition to include a wonderful survivor of the semaphore age along with 50015 Valiant pulling up at Newton Abbot on her way from Paddington to Penzance on 17 September 1983. **Barrie Renwick**

Opposite: Still controlling the now albeit reduced signalling and track layout here at Newton Abbot since their heyday were two signal boxes, one at each end of the station, both can be picked out here as 50011 Centurion continues her journey westwards on 18 September 1983 with a Paddington to Penzance working. **Barrie Renwick**

Our determined cameraman is braving the incoming tide this time to bring us this shot of 50009 Conquerer slowing for the Dawlish stop on 22 September 1983. Today she will take this Plymouth to Edinburgh & Glasgow working as far north as Birmingham New Street, meanwhile the foaming sea encroaches up the beach. **Barrie Renwick**

Opposite: In May 1980, 50013 Agincourt found itself as the sixth and last Class 50 to be released back into regular traffic from its Doncaster refurbishment still in Rail Blue, thereafter Large Logo would be the order of the day. Therefore, on 1 December 1983 she almost made a refreshing change away from then now more commonplace newer livery locomotives as she races past South Moreton to the east of Didcot, having just joined the main Bristol to London line with her 11.15 Oxford to Paddington service. Little did any of us know that Agincourt would become the third of the class to be withdrawn on 6 April just five years later. *Martin Loader*

Right: A good choice of lens coupled with good fortune to have the two trains in frame at the same time on a sunny afternoon being spent at Cholsey on 14 April 1984. Coming up fast is 50016 Barham with the 14.15 Oxford to Paddington, while a Class 117/121 DMU combination brings up the rear with the earlier 13.40 Oxford to Paddington stopper. *Martin Loader*

Breaking the peaceful birdsong entertaining St. Austell's waiting passengers on a sunny 19 June 1984, 50008 Thunderer draws in with the 09.36 Liverpool to Penzance service. *Andy Stace*

Meanwhile also taken the same day was this view of 50044 Exeter bringing the stock making up the last leg of the Torbay Express away from Torquay on 19 June 1984. *Barrie Renwick*

Snaking through the reverse curves on the western approaches to Taunton on 20 June 1984 was 50031 Hood, she has been sent out today with the opening leg of this epic Penzance to Glasgow and Aberdeen working as far as Birmingham New Street. *Barrie Renwick*

Opposite: Back at Doncaster Works after being the fourth of just six of her class to be refurbished and originally put back to work still in Rail Blue, 50001 Dreadnought has come back for overhaul again, only by this time on 29 July 1984 Large Logo liveries were all the rage. *Strathwood Library Collection*

Opposite: The first few months of 1985 were sunny and cold providing good opportunities for photography for those willing to brave the elements. Here we see 50033 Glorious well into her stride as she passes the remnants of a recent snowfall near Hayes with a down express. *Chris Wilson Collection*

The sun is shining again, and it is much warmer by 19 June 1985 to take up a suitable position to photograph 50049 Defiance near Paignton arriving from Newton Abbot. *Barrie Renwick*

These nine coaches are hardly going to tax 50035 Ark Royal as she departs from Dawlish westwards along the reasonably level coastal section of line hugging the seashore on 1 July 1985. However just eleven miles further along the route after leaving Newton Abbot and we are into the third steepest mainline bank on the British mainland, with two miles varying between 1 in 36 and 1 in 57. By the time that 50005 Collingwood was seen leaving Dainton's smoky tunnel on 2 July 1985, the driver of this Paddington to Penzance duty was now pushing his locomotive to the limit. The climb proper began at Stoneycombe and continued through Dainton Tunnel to the signal box on the right, a distance of 2 miles and 17 chains.
Both: Barrie Renwick

Opposite: Many would disagree perhaps but surely black was a more sensible colour to paint the roofline of Class 50s in Large Logo livery due to their smoky sooty habits. As witnessed by 50028 Tiger quietly stalking its next train at Birmingham New Street during October 1985. *David T. Williams*

This is clear to see the following year as we watch 50033 Glorious storming away from Waterloo and into Vauxhall station with the 11.10 departure for Exeter on 17 March 1986. Her roof being now black with sooty deposits rather than paint in this instance.
Strathwood Library Collection

The inclusion of a GUV in the formation immediately gives a clue to the destination of this train, as 50018 Resolution approaches Hinksey on 21 June 1986 at the head of the 17.07 Paddington to Hereford service. Even without reference to the timetable of the day, the presence of a van in the formation instantly identifies this as a Cotswold Line service, rather than one of the numerous London to Oxford trains, which were also capably hauled by Class 50s at this time. *Martin Loader*

Another alternative to improve the public's perception of the cleanliness of 50006 Neptune was to go for a dark grey roof with black headcode boxes as seen entering Par with a Plymouth to Penzance stopper on 12 May 1986. *Barrie Renwick*

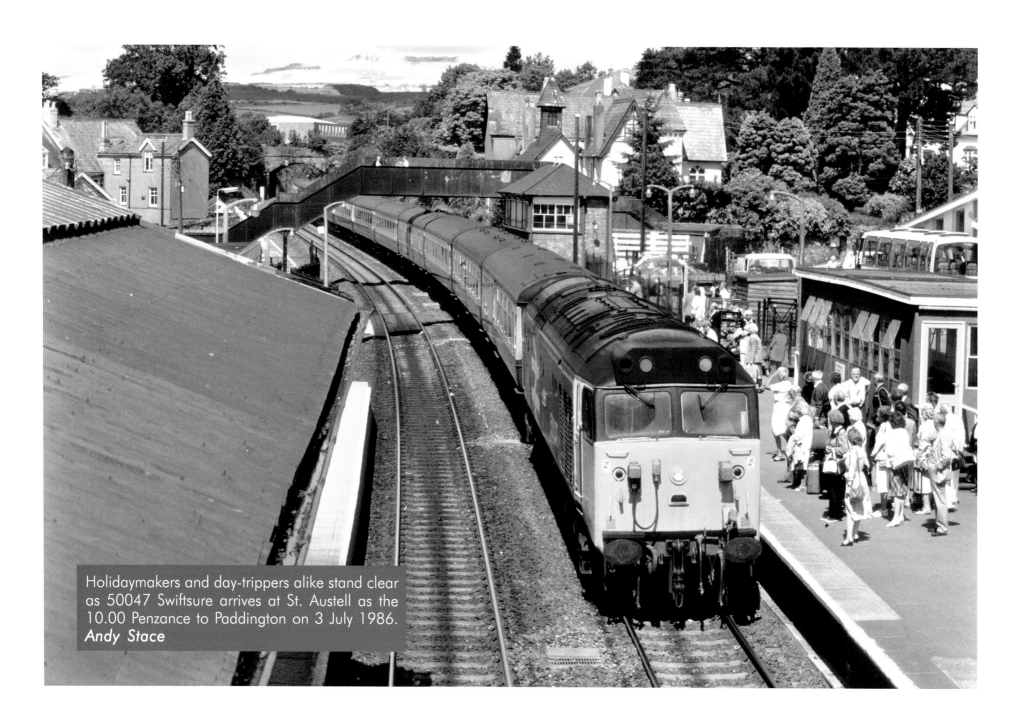

Holidaymakers and day-trippers alike stand clear as 50047 Swiftsure arrives at St. Austell as the 10.00 Penzance to Paddington on 3 July 1986.
Andy Stace

With the bracket signalling at Par suitably positioned to be easily sighted off the curve, 50011 Centurion appears once again this time with a Newquay service on 20 September 1986. *Barrie Renwick*

Another carefully planned exposure to record 50015 Valiant near St. Blazey coming to the end of the Newquay branch with a service bound for Newcastle on 20 September 1986. With it still being such a lovely warm day, several lads cannot resist hanging out of the windows to enjoy the sound of this Class 50 at work, who can blame them? *Barrie Renwick*

An easy race perhaps, as 50001 Dreadnought runs parallel with a Mk2 Ford Escort estate on the approaches to Coombe with the 08.00 Hereford to Paddington service on 4 October 1986. Although by this date Network SouthEast had been launched, the Cotswold Line was still predominantly Rail Blue, with just one of the new Inter City branded coaches breaking up the uniformity here. *Martin Loader*

Another case of careful composition and execution were required for both of these shots too by another talented cameraman. Nicely framed by this tree alongside the line near Baulking between Swindon and Didcot on 10 December 1986, 50048 Dauntless was captured as the motive power of the 08.36 Cheltenham to Paddington. *Martin Loader*

Crossing Frampton Mansell viaduct with the same 08.36 Cheltenham to Paddington working a few months later on 11 April 1987 was 50034 Furious now in her first Network SouthEast guise. *Martin Loader*

Cars and BRUTE trolleys of the day stand alongside the platforms here at Worcester's Shrub Hill station on 19 April 1987 as 50010 Monarch has been signalled away beneath those attractive Western Region style of lower quadrants. *Colour Rail*

The rather prominent large diamond shaped badge above the nameplate of 50008 Thunderer stands proudly here as she passes Aller Junction with a Swindon to Penzance service on 21 April 1987. This had been fitted during August 1986 replacing a smaller circular Royal Navy badge that had been awarded to the locomotive previously in September 1979. HMS Thunderer was the fourth and last Orion-Class dreadnought battleship to be built for the Royal Navy almost seventy years previously. *Andy Stace*

Aside from the much brighter new 'toothpaste' style of Network SouthEast livery branding to be seen on the other side of the bridge here at Aller Junction the following day, we can also see the need to move the positioning of the locomotive's nameplates to suit, as worn by 50026 Indomitable running light on 22 April 1987. At this point the first of the class was already withdrawn as 50011 Centurion lay dumped at Crewe Works. *Colour Rail*

Opposite: Climbing up the 1 in 65 incline into Bodmin Parkway on 24 June 1987, 50029 Renown makes a refreshing and powerful sight in her recently applied Network SouthEast colours, although hardly on NSE territory with this Penzance to Glasgow parcels working. *Barrie Renwick*

A return to the same location two weeks later brings us 50010 Monarch also approaching Bodmin Parkway this time with the 09.11 Penzance to Plymouth on 7 July 1987. Although it is only a Type 2 load for a Type 4 locomotive though today. *Andy Stace*

It gets worse, as consecutively numbered 50002 Superb and 50003 Temeraire are seen leaving Oxford with a ridiculously easy load on 26 July 1987. This is the 09.00 Oxford to Old Oak Common empty newspaper vans. In truth this was a working booked for double headed Class 50s purely as a balancing move. *Martin Loader*

Opposite: A far cry from their days working longer distances between Crewe and Glasgow on Anglo-Scottish expresses, as 50025 Invincible raises the echoes early one summer morning in the Avon Valley as she heads north past Limpley Stoke with the 06.55 Yeovil Pen Mill to Bristol Temple Meads service on 15 August 1987. *Rail Photoprints*

The driver of this Penzance to Edinburgh working cannot resist a sideways glance across to his home depot at Long Rock as he powers 50037 Illustrious away hard along the level section departing from Penzance on 30 August 1987. Very soon this will become a working in the hands of HSTs.
Barrie Renwick

Opposite: With Restormel Castle and the River Fowey behind us, 50017 Royal Oak starts the climb away from Lostwithiel towards Treverrin Tunnel on 5 September 1987 with a Paddington to Newquay working, loaded to just five coaches today.
Barrie Renwick

Opposite: Our intrepid photographer certainly did his best to bring us this lovely, elevated view over Starcross station on 1 October 1987 just as 50032 Courageous complete with her black backed nameplates and badges brings today's Penzance bound Cornish Scot through non-stop. Look back at page 8 to work out where Barrie was positioned. *Barrie Renwick*

Another elevated view, this time from the signal box over-looking Waterloo station a short while later during October 1987, as the former 50007 Hercules now with full celebrity status in Great Western Railway green livery as Sir Edward Elgar, performs a light engine movement appropriately at the London terminus. *Graham Wareham*

Not much further to go for the hulk of 50006 Neptune when it was tracked down within the busy scrapyard of Vic Berry in Leicester on 19 February 1988. She had been taken out of service officially on 20 July 1987. When the refurbishment programme originally started, she had been the first to be released back into service during November 1979. *Richard Lillie*

Imagine the rumbling noises from this motley rake of assorted empty ballast wagons coming off Brunel's famous bridge across the River Tamar at Saltash on 24 April 1988. The driver of 50027 Lion making very sure he does not exceed the 15mph speed limit on the bridge. *Colour Rail*

This would have been a great spot for these two young lads to while away the day in their shorts, enjoying both train spotting and taking their photographs on such a lovely sunny day. However, in this instance our talented cameraman has gone for the more elevated view from the roadway to include the human interest as 50018 Resolution pops back into the sunlight from the tunnel at Coryton Cove on 6 August 1988. As the Class 50 teasingly hugs the coastline here on its way from Paddington to Penzance. *Barrie Renwick*

Taking the ex-London & South Western Railway's route to Devon a few days later on 8 August 1988 we catch sight of 50027 Lion snaking its way towards Honiton with a Waterloo to Exeter working along a section that was once double tracked, such was the passenger volume and the number of services required especially during the summer months. *Barrie Renwick*

Opposite: The two railmen discuss the whereabouts for this rake of platform trolleys on 15 September 1988 almost oblivious to the passage of 50002 Superb passing through Exeter St. David's with the ecs for the next Waterloo service today. *Barrie Renwick*

Another through working five days later with the Southern Region on 20 September 1988 is seen near Totnes behind 50001 Dreadnought, with a Portsmouth to Plymouth service. The newer revised Network SouthEast livery now adding further to the livery mix. *Barrie Renwick*

Opposite: In a further livery blend to be enjoyed while holidaying in Devon & Cornwall that September we see 50017 Royal Oak and 50015 Valiant making a double-headed light engine move through Lostwithiel on 22 September 1988. We are not sure if this were to reduce line occupation or as a result of 50015's failure. *Barrie Renwick*

Another goal for this trip was to photograph 50149 Defiance in her unique grey livery, albeit now looking scruffy and well coated with china clay dust no doubt as she was tracked down near Carne Point the same day on the Lostwithiel to Fowey branch. *Barrie Renwick*

Looking very respectable and smart and retaining her Large Logo livery 50033 Glorious comes off her train at Reading in October 1988. During 1987, 50006/11/14 had all been withdrawn, then during 1988 it had been the turn for a further five locomotives with 50010/13/22/38/47 all being taken out of traffic. By 18 March 1989, two of these 50013 and 50038 the erstwhile Agincourt and Formidable were sorry looking specimens indeed after having been heavily robbed of spares here at Old Oak Common. Both would be partly cut up here and finished off completely at Vic Berry's premises in Leicester that summer. *Photos: Strathwood Library Collection & Russell Watkins*

Opposite: Improvements of the public's opinion of the railways were certainly achieved at the time, once the station and rolling stock repaints along with the modernisation enhancements took a hold for Network SouthEast. This is 50035 Ark Royal arriving at Twyford with a down stopper in April 1989, doing its bit to raise the bar a little from the previous low point a decade beforehand.
Strathwood Library Collection

Although this colourful new image Network SouthEast was attempting to portray was sometimes let down by the many years of neglect that had gone beforehand, such as here at Clapham Junction. Even though it was the country's busiest station for train movements as demonstrated in this scene as a Class 73 on an up train passes 50003 Temeraire with a down Exeter train on 26 May 1989. *Barrie Renwick*

A rare appearance for 50019 Ramillies in its Laira Blue livery to Oxford's Hinksey Yard on 23 July 1989, with an engineer's working. *Martin Loader*

This was a great time for fans of subtle livery variations too such as the red buffer beams on 50036 Victorious passing Waltham St. Lawrence on 2 June 1989, or the black backed nameplates of 50032 Courageous now without its badges making this stop at Reading with a Bristol to Paddington train on 20 July 1989.

Photos: Martin Loader & Barrie Renwick

Thankfully, accidents involving Class 50s were a rarity, on 23 November 1983, a sleeper train hauled by 50041 Bulwark was derailed onto its side approaching Paddington due to excessive speed through a crossover. Amazingly just three of the seventy passengers onboard were injured, and the locomotive was returned to service after major repairs at Doncaster. Next was to happen on 6 August 1989, as 50025 Invincible was derailed at West Ealing whilst hauling the 21.15 Oxford to Paddington service. The cause was a length of rail that vandals had placed across the track. There were no fatalities, but as we see here it was certainly enough to finish off the locomotive, despite its name. She would be scrapped by staff from Vic Berry Ltd at Old Oak Common in October that year. *Grahame Wareham*

Unusual perhaps to be this way around, but 50016 Barham has the failed 33208 in tow, between Fisherton Tunnel and Salisbury's station on 19 August 1989. *Barrie Renwick*

Opposite: Although the original version of Network SouthEast livery did not wear so well in traffic, the same must be said really that the revised version also fared little better, as worn by 50001 Dreadnought shuffling about light engine within the station limits at Exeter St. David's on 17 September 1989. *Barrie Renwick*

With another Class 50 departure to follow 50045 away from Salisbury on 19 August 1989, we can see that her Achilles nameplate is missing as she heads away first with an Exeter to Waterloo train. She had been named as Achilles originally on 12 April 1978, at Plymouth's Laira depot without ceremony. *Barrie Renwick*

Several NSE combinations to enjoy firstly with 50035 Ark Royal going well near Goring on 25 September 1989 on its way from Oxford to Paddington. Next, we see 50034 Furious approaching Didcot North Junction on 26 November 1989, likewise with another Oxford to Paddington working. This one was booked to be a double header, sometimes as two Class 50s or a Class 47/50 combination or as here sometimes just as a single Class 50. In the following year we find 50034 Furious still at work on these services, this time passing Lower Basildon on 28 April 1990 with the 13.00 departure from Oxford, but this time looking like she might be in a spot of bother from her exhaust.

Photos: Barrie Renwick, Martin Loader & Rail Photoprints

Opposite: A totally unrepeatable sight from 6 July 1990 as DCWA allocated 50042 Triumph moves slowly out of the permanent way yard at Ashton Gate and heads for Bristol East Depot with the Severn Tunnel inspection train. This was one a handful of departmental allocated Class 50s that spent 1989 and 1990 pottering around on workings such as this. Even with its maintenance needs the Severn Tunnel has often been regarded as having represented the crowning achievement of the noted Victorian civil engineer and the GWR's chief engineer Sir John Hawkshaw. *Martin Loader*

The surviving members of the class were now starting to suffer from some serious reliability issues as the Class 50s were not suitable for the stop-start service pattern of Waterloo to Exeter services, couple this with the extended single-line sections of the route, where a single locomotive failure could cause chaos. Illustrated here with 50024 Vanguard piloting the failed 50003 Temeraire after it had died near Tisbury on this Exeter bound service on 20 July 1990. Ultimately the decision was taken to retire the fleet, temporarily replacing them with Class 47/7 locomotives. *Barrie Renwick*

With an ever-changing skyline in the background 50024 Vanguard passes the civil engineering yard at Woking on 26 July 1990 on its way from Waterloo to Salisbury. *Barrie Renwick*

The persistent problem associated with the NSE makeover of both rolling stock and stations alike was the tendency for the colours to fade quickly. Such as here at West Byfleet on 26 July 1990 with 50003 Temeraire fit and working once again with an afternoon Waterloo to Exeter service. **Barrie Renwick**

During 1990 a further fourteen Class 50s succumbed to withdrawal including 50004/5/16/19/20/21/23/26/32/34/35/41/42/45. Early in 1991 during February, the flying cutters from Cooper's Metals descended upon Old Oak Common to scrap 50005/9/24/32/34/39/41 all onsite here around the turntable as we see 50034 Furious being put to the torch that month. *Strathwood Library Collection*

Meanwhile, the survivors soldiered on such as 50037 Illustrious as she takes the Salisbury line at Battledown Flyover with the 14.37 Basingstoke to Exeter service, which on 30 March 1991 had started at Basingstoke because of re-signalling work taking place at Waterloo. The end was nigh for this example too as she was withdrawn from traffic less than six months later on 9 September. Although in this case she would head back one last time to Glasgow for her scrapping at M.C. Metals the following year. Likewise, four more Class 50s 50003/18/46/48 would also get a final fling in the same Scottish scrapyard. *Rail Photoprints*

Enthusiast tours brought pairings such as 50008 Thunderer and 50015 Valiant together on 4 May 1991, as they draw admiring glances from both the rail tour passengers on the platform, and from passers by on the road above. They will soon set off from here at Penzance with the Pathfinder Tours 'Cornish Centurion 2' rail tour heading back to Manchester Piccadilly, although it was 47972 that handled the legs between Bristol and Manchester both ways. *Martin Loader*

As cameramen sought to grab as many shots as they could of Class 50s, some found new photographic locations such as St. Mary Bourne between Overton and Andover to record 50048 Dauntless in action still on 10 May 1991, with a Waterloo to Salisbury service. *Barrie Renwick*

Likewise, still hard at work out of Waterloo was 50002 Superb on 2 July 1991 just two months off being withdrawn, but out today on its way to Exeter when seen passing Pirbright at speed. *Barrie Renwick*

After all the efforts to promote NSE we still saw workings like this with Large Logo liveried 50046 Ajax starting to look tatty running fast through Winchfield on 24 July 1991, with a Yeovil Junction to Waterloo job. *Barrie Renwick*

Opposite: With sponsorship from enthusiasts, British Rail retro painted D400 which threw a further mix back in onto the Exeter to Waterloo route, that is when it was not out on rail tour duty itself. On 1 August 1991, she was seen hauling a full NSE rake up the last few yards of the 1 in 37 bank from Exeter St. David's into the city's Central station for the one hundred and seventy two mile run to Waterloo. *Barrie Renwick*

Also, still at work on 26 September 1991 on the route to Waterloo was 50046 Ajax, she would not bow out finally until 25 March the following year. By the start of 1992 though, just eight Class 50s remained in service, these being 50007/8/15/29/30/33/46/50. There would be no reprieve for Ajax upon withdrawal as she went to M.C. Metals in Glasgow who had cut her up by the end of June 1992. *Barrie Renwick*

Among the flurry of rail tours that were also being run to help raise funds for preservation was the Pathfinder Tours, 'Hoovering Druid' heading for Ebbw Vale. The train set off very early on 4 April 1992 from Manchester Piccadilly at 06.05 with 47574 up front as far as Derby. Then both 50033 Glorious and D400 were put on instead heading off via Birmingham, Gloucester and Cardiff. We catch the ensemble heading for Pontycymer at the head of the valley as they pass Pant-y-Gog. In the rear is 37212 adding to the sounds of the exhausts which have caught the attention of a few locals.
Martin Loader

Incredible crowds had greeted the 'Carlisle Fifty' rail tour upon its arrival from Waterloo on 11 April 1992. Both celebrity Class 50s, D400 & 50007 Sir Edward Elgar worked the tour throughout, here they parallel the M6 motorway at Dillicar on their return journey. Popularity for the class, saw 402 making its preservation debut at the Paignton & Dartmouth Railway's 'Diesel Gala' weekend on 20 June 1992. Arriving at Kingswear with the 10.20 service from Paignton, the locomotive had been withdrawn from mainline use the previous September. *Both: Martin Loader*

Left: This tour behind D400 & 50007 Sir Edward Elgar on 23 January 1993 was already running 35 minutes late as it stood at Hereford, it would be delayed even further afterwards on its return to Manchester Piccadilly as it encountered sheep on the line near Abergavenny. *Martin Loader*

Below: The prospect of triple-headed Class 50s brought enthusiasts out to the lineside to see and hear 8,100hp in action as the colourful formation of 50033 Glorious, D400 and 50007 Sir Edward Elgar pass Bromford Bridge on the 'Bishop's Triple' rail tour on 5 June 1993. *Antony Guppy*

The Paignton & Dartmouth Railway's 'Class 50 Day' on 16 October 1993 saw 50007 Sir Edward Elgar and 50033 Glorious double-heading to the joy of their passengers as they cross Hookhills Viaduct. Also, in action was 50002 Superb climbing Goodrington Bank during the same event. *Both: Martin Loader*

Above: Back on their old stomping ground on 30 October 1993, 50033 Glorious and 50007 Sir Edward Elgar speed past Winwick bound for Bristol with the 'Merseyman' rail tour. In the background to the right of the pylon above 50007 is the birthplace of the Class 50s, English Electric's Vulcan Foundry.

Left: Pouring rain does little to deter photographers at Penzance on 19 March 1994 after the arrival of 50033 Glorious and 50050 Fearless, both once again back in Large Logo livery with the 'Cornish Caper' rail tour.
Both: Martin Loader

From those final eight locomotives starting 1992, three were kept on until 1994 for use on special rail tours, these being 50007 Sir Edward Elgar, 50033 Glorious along with 50050 Fearless (D400). The former 50007 had been returned to working order using parts from 50046 Ajax, which surrendered its recently overhauled power unit and bogies too. By this time, 50050 had been repainted into Large Logo livery and 50007 also received a repaint into GWR green as the 1985 paint was wearing very thin. The final rail tours operated in March 1994, during one of which 50033 was delivered for preservation at the National Railway Museum. The final rail tour was operated with 50007 and 50050 from Waterloo to Penzance and returned to London at Paddington. This was the Pathfinder Tours '50 Terminator' seen passing Totnes on 26 March 1994, after which both locomotives were sold into preservation. *Martin Loader*

For our finale we have chosen this 6 August 1994 shot of the preserved 50031 Hood at Kidderminster on the Severn Valley Railway beautifully restored complete with a blue painted roof as uniquely carried by 50010 Monarch when in mainline British Rail service.
Martin Loader